The Whispers

of

Pow Chin Chew

The Whispers of

Pow Chin Chew

by
Eddie Morales

Copyright © 2017 Eddie Morales

All rights reserved

ISBN 13:   978-1938094088

Contents

Introduction	1
Pow Chin Chew	2
Apples	3
Friends	4
Purpose	5
Travel	6
All	7
Enjoy	8
Language	9
Path	10
Choice	11
Treespeak	12
Fearless	13
Witness	14
Deities	15
Inevitability	16
Contemplation	17
Beauty	18
Forever	19
Faithful	20
Standing	21
Songsters	22
Oaks	23
Happiness	24

Observation	25
Humor	26
The Human Poem by Poetree	27
Tag	28
Sharing	29
Scenery	30
Natural	31
Red	32
Magnificence	33
Hibernation	34
Far	35
Dance	36
Busy	37
Bloom	38
Lost	39
Progression	40
Recipe	41
Source	42
Ado	43
Sunbathing	44
Matcher	45
Rendezvous	46
Party	47
Palms	48
Failed	49

Nighttime	50
Range	51
Ego	52
Divine	53
Soul	54
Beacon	55
Sadness	56
Talent	57
Life	58
Secret	59
Spring	60
Summer	61
Autumn	62
Winter	63
Transition	64
Blind	65
Be	66
Seasons	67
Knowing	68
Enlightenment	69
Unknown	70
Finite	71
Monsters	72
Family	76
Say	77

Adage	78
Progeny	79
Eye	80
Honor	81
Unity	82
Raincheck	83
Offspring	84
Eternity	85
OTHER BOOKS BY THE AUTHOR	87

Introduction

The inspiration for this book comes mainly from the Haiku, Senryu, and Tanka. Add a little dash of: Zen, Hindu, Asian, Confucius, and Persian ingredients and you have what I call a *whisper*.

Before I explain a whisper picture this: You are a child sitting at the dinner table picking at your food. Your mother sees you doing this and she comes up behind you and smacks you on the back of your head. She then tells you to stop picking at your food and eat.

This scene is an actual scene from childhood, where my mother would sometimes tap me, or my sister or brother, on the back of the head when she thought we were not eating fast enough and would tell us to hurry up.

Well for some reason this moment in my life popped into my head and I think it is what set the stage for this book. It gave me the title for this book as I thought about my childhood memory. My siblings and I would talk about what my mother did to us a dinnertime and joke about it. We might say something like, "Better hurry up and eat or mom is going to POW you on the back of your head."

It was a term we learned from comic books this *POW*, when the good guys would fight with the bad guys and it was, *Pow! Zing! Crunch! Thud!* etc. So, POW is what we called my mother's tap on the back of our heads. So, I used this POW as something that makes you think twice and get on with it. Think of POW as that epiphany, that realization, that idea at the back of your head which comes to the forefront and makes you think of something you had not thought of before. The light bulb that turns on when you get an idea.

Taking this one step further, I thought what my mother was trying to say to us was to make our chins move and get on with our chewing our food and finish eating. With that thought came *my* epiphany for: Pow Chin Chew. That was going to be the *persona* for my book.

The name makes sense at least to me. We often say things like, "Chew on that," "Let's chew the fat," or "Taking it on the chin." It had nothing to do with the Asian names Chin or Chiu, although, because of the Asian sounding name of Pow Chin Chew, which I guess I could change to Pau Chin Chiu, I could make the transition to a human persona, and I thought of doing that. Until I searched for a picture to use on the cover of my book and I saw the tree which I finally used for my book.

The tree I used for the cover then gave me the name for the type of poem I wanted to create. Having sat under many a tree myself, I often thought the tree, when a gentle breeze blows through its branches, whispers to me. If I use the tree as my persona, then it was logical that if a tree was going to actually speak to me, it would do so in whispers. Ergo, the title, *The Whispers of Pow Chin Chew*. We have horse whisperers and dog whisperers, why not a tree that whispers?

So now we get to the whisper itself. This is easy. Anything you would say in a haiku, senryu, or tanka can be said in a whisper. You can take as many lines to say it from the three-line haiku to the seven-line tanka or use all three forms in a single poem or as many lines as would fit on the page used in a 6x9 book of poetry, broken up into any form you want.

In Japan a haiku is written as one line which has seventeen syllables. The first five syllables present an image of nature while the next seven syllables give an image of time, and the last five syllables may present a link between the first two images, or creates an entirely different image. In English haiku, we use three lines in order to make it easier to present the three images presented in a poem written in Japanese.

In short, write anything you would write in any of the forms I have discussed. Meld them together, use them separately, use one and not the others, use them all except one, there is no wrong way to use them. If you want to create your own whisper, let's say using a cat as your persona, then you would write your poems as if the cat were speaking to you. Or you can use a dog as your persona, or an Orangutan if you wish.

When you read these poems, you will see that almost all of the titles to the poems are one-word titles. This is intentional. Haiku, senryu, and tanka are usually presented with no titles. I decided to use one-word titles because I wanted to hint at what the poem is about through a title. I also wanted to use the title as part of the whisper.

Look at the title of each poem in this book and think of what other word or words could be associated with that one word. For example, if I use the title *Range*, you might think of a stove, or home on the range, or open range. If I use the title *Red*, you might think Blood Red, or Red Blooded, or Red Tape, etc. The title may or may not seem to have anything to do with the poem, but even a title that doesn't seem to belong to the poem may actually be hinting at the opposite of what the poem is saying.

As for the meanings of the poems, I can't help you with that. Like the haiku, senryu, or tanka, the author presents you with the words, the images, and leaves you, the reader, to put them together as you see fit. You must make the connections for yourself. However, a good discussion of the poem might reveal other connections I may not have seen myself. Sounds like something worthwhile doing to me.

Also, there are no punctuation marks or contractions in a whisper. Although there are no question or quotation marks either, you will have no problem knowing where they go. As for the *Dauphin* font, it seemed to me to be appropriate for the whisper.

Oh, one last thing. Your whispers must not come from any human being. However, if you want to use an inanimate object you can. Now, let us hear the whispers.

The Whispers

of

Pow Chin Chew

Pow Chin Chew

I am the tree
Pow Chin Chew
My name is unimportant
That I am a tree is

I represent life

I live
I will die

Your name is not important
That you are you is

You live
You will die

Therefore Nature will not
do you nor I any favors

Apples
The apple holds no knowledge
and eating it will not disgrace you

Disgraceful it would be to shun
the gift which Nature offers you

It is nourishment for the body but
be careful to return the seeds to earth

because the Apple Tree knows all
there is to know lies inside the seeds

Friends

Seeing you standing before me
empty handed makes you my friend

If you bring a rope I will give you
pleasure by holding the swing for you

But if the rope you bring has a noose
I can no longer be your friend

Nature forbids it

Purpose

If I am gladly in your way
then cut me down

Use my body to build your shelter
and I will be happy to protect you

Use my body to make your table
and I will be with you at mealtimes

Use my body to make your cup
and I will always drink with you

Cut me down for no reason
and my memory is gone forever

Travel

See the world

Seek all there is to seek
and see all there is to see

Do all there is to do
Laugh as much as you can
Be sad when you are sad

Share all you have
with those you hold most dear

Then come and share with me
all you have seen and done
So I too may know the world

All

Make yourself one with the universe
and you will go beyond the limits of
possible experience and knowledge

Transcendence will disappear because
it will remain with the physical world

When transcendence vanishes
the true you will appear

Then you are one with your all

Start out as an empty vessel
and let what is divine work

I know what is divine
because I have gazed upon the stars

Enjoy

You are the universe

>It is within you
>It is without you

It is here
and it is everywhere else

Seek the life force but only when it is time
otherwise you will not get to enjoy
all there is to enjoy here

I am standing here waiting for you
to arrive

The joy is not for me
It is for you

Language
I have suffered the arrows of your
injustice upon my bark

I have held the rope of your racism
with my limbs

I have felt the letters you have carved
on my flesh when you thought you
were in love

The joy of doves hides amongst my leaves

Neither the dove nor I object to
anything you do

We do not object
because
we do not speak your language

You do not listen to each other anyway

Path

Being human is different
than being a tree

Being a tree is different
than being human

It depends on the path you take

If you take the path that leads away from the tree
you will see the world

If you take the path that leads to the tree
you will see the universe

Choice

You ask if I am weak
and I am

Your axe makes me weak

You ask if I am strong
and I am

Your love for me makes me strong

This is not difficult to see

Choose which one
you want me to be

Treespeak

I get my fire from sun
I get my strength from soil
I get my essence from water
Then I use air to speak

When the Zephyr travels through
my leaves you should listen to what
I have to say

Fearless
I am grateful to whomever comes

Therefore

I will be the shade

        protect against rain

        protect against sun

I will be the leaning post to rest upon

I will always stand by you
and never run away in fear

For I do not know what fear is
even when I see Death

His is just another face and
I am grateful

Witness

Did you run to get beneath my limbs
in order to feel safe

Did you hear the guns firing and hide
behind the thickness of my body

Were you with me for the lynching

Were you with me for the war

I have witnessed much
for having traveled nowhere

Deities
If there is a God
there is one

If there are gods
there are many

Which is yours depends on what you believe

I do not believe
I simply am
which makes me better at living in peace

Yet

Something beyond us
governs both our lives

Inevitability

I see the fire coming and
there is nothing to do but wait

The tornado is on its way and
there is nothing to do but wait

You must run and leave me
behind to be consumed

I consume water, metals,
and nutrients to survive

The fire needs to eat as well
The tornado must rage as well

and I must oblige if I am in their way

Contemplation
When you are beneath me
and I whisper in your ear

The whisperings take you to other places
to other conversations

sometimes angry
sometimes melancholy
sometimes fearful
sometimes hateful

And then there are the happy thoughts
of love
of friendship
of family

And suddenly I feel for the Oak
and Weeping Willow

Beauty

Plum-blossoms are a gift
and gazing upon them
honors the tree

The beauty of a woman
is like that of the Plum-blossom

and a man should look to honor the
parents of such a woman
by gazing upon her beauty

You will never see ugliness if
you look not with your eyes

Forever
There exists all there is
divided between yesterday
today and tomorrow

We travel through them
no matter where you have been
where you are
or where you will be

The path is simple
Today will be yesterday tomorrow

It is the path to eternity

Faithful
I do not belong to the day
I do not belong to the afternoon
I do not belong to the night

They all belong to me

The sun must rise when I awaken
The afternoon must walk along with me
And the night must arrive when I sleep

You decide which part of me
most suits your needs

I am not going anywhere

Standing

The puppy that does not know
my bark will be happy to test it

The dog that knows my bark will
be glad for the scent of an old friend

The old dog will be grateful if
I watch over him when he dies

Songsters

The crows came with a great raucous
and sang a very coarse song

Then the Blue Jays arrived and sang an angry
song to see if the crows would return their eggs

Then they both left and the Nightingales
came to sing their most beautiful songs

And when they were all gone
you came to sit beside me

and the obliging breeze helped
me whisper a soothing song for you

Oaks

The Oak represents power
The Oak is a symbol of survival
The Oak possesses Ancient Wisdom

He demonstrates these qualities
by never leaving his post

Happiness

The spraying of an evening shower
to cool the heat of the body

The family picnic beneath my hat
while the ants enjoy what they
can get away with

Lovers forgetting I am watching

The babies the lovers later bring
is the favorite of the Willow

It makes her weep for joy

Observation
We are all busy doing what
we are supposed to be doing

The spider spinning
The boll weeviling
The bees beeing
The fly flying
The ants hilling

I watch
I am the watcher watching

Humor

First it was the little twig
the Apple Tree dropped

Then it was the larger twig
then the sprinkling of leaves

And although dropping the apple
did give Newton his idea

Newton failed to see
the humorous side

He could have been sitting
under a Coconut Tree

The Human Poem by Poetree

I think that I will never see
a creature uglier to me
You sit beside me face all pressed
against a thing you call a breast
A breast you like to see each day
and beg her sister join the play
Upon her bosom you have lain
quite intimately beneath the rain
I may have robins nest my hair
but they make lovely summer wear
Poem my Nature made tis true
but as a joke your God made you

Tag

I run to the top of the hill and
I shake my Oak leaves tauntingly

The Poplars start hopping
towards the top of the hill

I run to the center of the valley
and shake my leaves again

The Poplars start hopping towards
the center of the valley

Finally I shake my leaves in laughter
at the top of the hill

I am too fast for the Poplars

Sharing

Share your chores
Share your meals
Share your days

Worship if you want to
Worship if you need to

Work enough to enjoy not working

I always do these things
and I am a happy tree

Scenery

hidden is the sun
winter stones ready to spring
when the feet of spring have sprung
stones ready to spring
transformation of white snow
soothing waters bring
transmuted white snow
bathing stones along the streams
branches overflow
bathing in the streams
winter sleeps while spring is sprung
sweet and balmy dreams
the young feet of spring have sprung
leaping over the warm stones
golden is the sun
but first run the stones
clear the path through fallen snow
warm my aching bones

Natural
The Orchids are in concert

The whippoorwills
sing in midnight harmony

Bullfrogs sing bass
under the silvery full moon

Go ahead and cry little baby

Red
So peaceful the sky
under the white clouds

A spotless white Dove flies

Out of the blue

dives the brown Hawk
and lands on her wings

I do not recognize this rain
which falls upon my limbs

Magnificence
I blew my moon a summer night kiss
and waited for one in return

Then a comet streaked through
the Milky Way

Asteroids lost their sense of direction
as they traveled between the stars

The heads of the planets turned

I know my moon loves me

Hibernation

Snow fallen several inches deep

Signs of bear in the white powder
causes a great commotion

Pine trees head for the hills
each hopping on one leg

A Weeping Willow sings to
the sleepy bear

Far

Go be with your friends
Maybe sit by the ocean

Sit on a hill
and feel the presence of
each other

Sit by a tree and
feel the presence of the

stars
moon
sun
sky

If you show up
you may just show up

And everything else will follow

Dance

I know how to dance the bolero
The cha-cha-cha
The merengue
The waltz

I have seen the motion of dancers
Synchronized heartbeats

Now teach me the samba

The Zephyr knows
I know
how to shake it

Busy
Bookstore mother drinks
hot tea at twenty thousand leagues

She has traveled the world
in eighty days

Paris lay before her at the turn of a page
while the children are home sound asleep

The days and nights of a tree
are indeed busy ones

Bloom

Reflections in her eyes
Reflections in my mind

Spring moonlight dinner

The awakening Orchid
opened her petals

I drank in her aroma
and she died with me

Lost

Better to walk alone than
in bad company

Better to sleep alone
than with a cutthroat

Better to ride alone than
with an assassin

Better to let a loved one
go if you truly love

It is easier to stop a salivating camel
from spitting

Progression

Life is geared to let things grow
physically and spiritually

If we stop growing physically
the body may still be able to
sustain life

But if we stop growing spiritually
we are as good as dead

A good acorn is born with this knowledge

Recipe

You must have
a good piece of heaven
a good piece of earth
and a great deal of human kindness

If you mix these ingredients
well there is cause for celebration
and there will be peace

It is all that is
true
good
and beautiful

Source
If you want to find the place
where all life began

Close your eyes

Go deep into the highest mountains
Go down to the deepest valleys

Take a deep breath of the universe
Breathe out the cosmos

Smell the aromas of what
nature provides

Come back to yourself
and there it is

Now open your eyes

Ado

So much to do today

The fingers of the Zephyr
must be ready to
play delicate music
on the scale of ripples on the pond

The North Wind was in a hurry
before dawn but I was there on time
when he almost knocked me down
as he flew past me

I made sure to set my clock so I would not
be late when the sun arrived

I must have the tire ready
for the kids to swing on

Then there is the picnic to prepare for

I have to get some sleep when the sun sets for
tomorrow I plan to be even busier

Sunbathing
Finally
some time to myself
to spread out my limbs
and face my leaves towards the sun

To soak up the moisture
from deep within the soil

To soak my Ashy roots in
the mud bath of the earth

Ah

The Tamarind looks awesome

Matcher

His lady is wearing green
and the Scarlet Tanager is in love

He is singing his heart out
by the side of the road

She is playing hard to get
but the nest is ready

I shake my Maple leaves

You may not see it
but I am smiling now

Rendezvous

Midnight tryst
under silver beams

So young
So young

Balmy air
Cool summer breeze
Flesh on fire
Sharing of forbidden fruits

Apple cores remain

Party

Come to me at midnight
when the moon is full

I will wear the
scariest of all costumes

My limb with five branches
will reach out to grab you

The moon between my
leaves will seem to give me eyes

The owl hiding in my
hair will seem to give me a voice

Then I will whisper
Welcome to my party

Palms

There is a moon over the ocean
and one atop the ocean itself
I can see clearly

I let my whispers wander across the sand
and they are met by the crashing tide

When no one is looking I sneak
across the sand and jump into the waves
for a while then I hurry back

Then my accomplice the sea
washes away my tree prints

So no one will ever know I can swim

Failed

Most of the time
I feel trains whistling happily

Sometimes through my roots
I can feel them rumbling sadly

One going east
One going west

Once in a while they pass
each other in the night

And I can feel they are both
headed in the wrong direction

Nighttime
Millions of stars in a cloudless sky
hold a place for the heroes of myth

The full moon shines its
light on the celestial stage

On earth

lightning bugs interpret
each constellation

Range
I used to feel the ground thunderously
shake they were so many

I could feel the hoofs
of horses chase after their sound

Arrows would streak
across the sky and shadow the sun

I feel no joy now from the silence

Ego
Though I have no lover
I am happy and I rejoice

I am very important
to the world

I must love myself
because Nature makes it so

I cannot defy my nature so
you will always see me as narcissistic

I cannot be otherwise
since I stand alone

Divine

If you want a god
you can have one

But you cannot see nor touch
the divine with your gross senses

Your ears will never hear
the divine

The divine will never
outwardly interfere with your life

These things are meant for your heart
mind and soul

Look inside yourself

Soul

My body has been useful
in the creation of a place of gathering

I have become stronger
standing by as your wall

as your roof

as your floor

I have become the table upon
which I have placed the
most flavorful bread and wine

Even if I am burnt to the ground
You will not die

Beacon

Do not be the rock that
sinks to the bottom of the ocean

Stay awake and be with your friend
and your friend will do the same

Crash against the rocks like the ocean
and do not let the hurricane take you

Somewhere in that dark ocean
is the flowing waters of life

And somewhere inside you
and your friend is the light

Sadness

The Sparrow flies into the North Wind
and freezes to death

and falls to the ground

The Oak trees bow their heads
to the sunset falling onto the graveyard

The wolf howls at the moon

The cat is happy

Talent
I have no talent

All I do is stand here
unable to go anywhere

When the lightning prepares to strike
I have no talent for avoiding its fire

If the tornado walks over me I have
no talent for fighting

If the chainsaw approaches
I have no talent for running

I will have to settle for being lovely

Life

You really do not know
everything there is to
know about me

I have all the wisdom of
the world inside me

I have all the mathematical
formulae of the universe
all figured out

I know how to create
every adaptation

You only know
the little I have given you

Secret

Something hides deep inside of me
and I have no power to tell you
what it is or where it came from

The rain falls upon the ground
and my roots know what to do

The sun beats down upon
my leaves and I know how to
be the master of the elements

Maybe you can figure out
all that I truly am

but I will never know
I know these things

Spring

At the first sign of spring
the Paulownia opens her
lavender flowers

When this Royal Empress
is watered the hummingbird appears

The hummingbird dances
without the need for music

The Oak tree is moved

This must be the way
Oak trees fall in love

Summer
Walk under the
Cherry Blossom tree
in the spring

Become part of her world

Nature painted her

Being is to be young
Consummation is necessary

Red
Yellow
Purple

Take her cherry
when summer arrives

Autumn

The roads are cold and lonely
and on the field my vigilance begins

A crow passes by occasionally
to tell me I am getting old

My leaves have fallen to the
ground and the wind scatters them about

A calico cat seems interested
in the movement of my fallen leaves

but

the fire crackles

Winter

The Noble Fir has a date
with a thing called Christmas
although why is beyond any tree

When the axe sank in
there was no way to cry out

Death without any good reason
puzzles the snow dog sniffing
for his tree

Transition

I stood alone and the
grass grew around me

The weeds came to take over
the field I was born in

Then some of my neighbors
were cut down in their prime

A house was built with the
fine pieces of their flesh

The weeds were driven away
and the grass grew again around me

I learned about dogs
cats and children
and family

I would not mind dying to become a home

Blind

I do not care if the Acer blushes
the color of maroon

or that the White Ash shows
rich shades of red
purple
yellow
and green

Or that the Quercus has
a scarlet presentation

That is a problem of humans
Trees are color blind

Be
The life of a tree is guided
by the laws of Nature

There is a formula to follow
and biology to obey

Nature simply says
Be

and takes care of the science

Seasons

With Winter's icy breath
silver moonbeams kill Autumn
with their frigid hands

Spring is on the trail
Revenge is sweet
Summer waits in turn

They all know Lazarus

Knowing
Knowledge is always in danger
of being taken away

It lives in the mind

What is unknown is beyond us
and it belongs to the soul

The mind will never know everything
and it will perish when you die

In death the soul will become all knowing

Enlightenment
I have no knowledge
yet I know all I need to know

I have no voice
yet I know I must speak when
the symbiotic breeze flows
past me

To lose the immaturity
of the acorn I must have the courage
to step into the light

I must obey the Law

Without the laws of Nature
I am useless

Unknown

The future is unknown
and it will always be so

What is discovered is
incorporated into what is known
and the unknown remains the same

If I were to see my future

the moment I see it
my future would change

and I am back to not knowing

Finite
When you die what is
natural will be over

The supernatural awaits
you when the soul moves on

You cannot return to the mortal
once that vessel is no more

Losing the vessel takes
the soul to eternity

So I better stand here for
as long as I can while I can

Monsters
A walk through the Oaks
or the Weeping Willows
which path is more
filled with fright

If the headstones are strewn
between the two
and the moon is
full and bright

If the Oaks are tall
and barren their boughs
their shadows bring
shudders to bear

While phantoms appear
to move through the dark
To raise every leaf of my hair

I move and they move
the arms of the Oaks
Then I hope the wind is to blame

But not the wind blows
not a whisper is heard

And I shiver away
just the same

So fancy and free
the wind then decides
To scurry the leaves about

The sound seems like
fire around my trunk
And I am anxious to
hurry on out

The moon is no help
casting slivers of light
Through the Weeping
Willows I am led

Their sigh their moans
their whispering noise
Are like voices
to stir up the dead

Are they speaking to me
I say to myself
Do they want me
to hear and reply

Most certain I am they
would call out my name
Were I at that moment to die

Then it dawns on me
why these Willows all weep
And these Oak Trees
are filled with hate

And a reason why
this graveyard is full
For many have passed
through its gate

A long time ago both
guilty and guiltless
More guiltless than
guilty I know

Were hanged from the
boughs of these mighty Oaks
And left there to swing to and fro

Much sooner than later
a man hangs still
Or a lady quits

kicking her heels

And many a soul
hang on to the bark
To tell the poor
Oak how it feels

So an Oak gets mad
for it feels the pain
Of an innocent
soul that dies

And a Willow cannot
help its empathy
So the Willow breaks
down and cries

Between the two it
is crystal clear
Which path is more
filled with fright

It is the path that winds
through heartless men
monsters
who scare the trees at night

Family

My roots are like your roots
My limbs are like your limbs

My roots tell you
who your ancestors were

My limbs tell you
who your children are

Nature says we are twins

Say
The life of a tree
is the life for me

The handsome pine
will never whine

The mighty Oak
is a funny bloke

The Cherry Blossom
has a hearty bosom

But that Carambola
is hard to rhyme

Adage

Pow Chin Chew has a saying

The tree who leaves
is not as important

as the tree who arrives

or the tree who stays

It is the same with people

Progeny
Within a tree
there is another tree

The tree on the outside
is called mortality

The tree on the inside
is called immortality

The death of both is called oblivion

Eye
The differences between the beauty
of a woman and the beauty of a tree
is that one is

skin deep
and the other is
bark deep

One may also possess inner beauty
while the other only has outer beauty

and because of the eye
you always love the tree

The tree does not see in vain

Honor

I have kept my post on the battlefield
while you fought your wars

I have raised my arms when the
storms came to slow them down for you

I provided my limbs when the waters
rose too high for you to walk the roads

My breaths have kept you alive

I am a soldier
Without soldiers
your world would perish

Unity

I spend the day pondering
and when the breeze fills me
I tell you what I think

Where I came from
Where I am going

My soul belongs somewhere else
and for certain I will go there again

The day I meet you there
you will realize I spoke the truth

One universe
One soul

Raincheck

I took the day
to wash my feet in the
river below the ground

I took a shower in the rain

The Zephyr came and blew
all of my green dry

When evening arrived
you stood me up

I cried like a Weeping Willow

Offspring

The tree that does not multiply
loses its essence

Without the seed the sun
will turn essence to dust

All strength will be returned
to the soil from whence it came

Water and sustenance alone
will not save the soul of the tree

Eternity
I am the tree
Pow Chin Chew

My name is unimportant
That we have shared this moment is

I represent life
I whisper

    Do not forget to live

Nature demands it

THE END

OTHER BOOKS BY THE AUTHOR

A Reason for Rhyme
ISBN 978-0615566924

The Suicide Sonnets
ISBN 978-1467931281

Count Edweird Lefang's Rhymin' Halloween (Funny Cover)
ISBN 978-0615565163

Count Edweird Lefang's Rhymin' Halloween (Signature Cover)
ISBN 978-1938094019

A Candle on Fire
ISBN 978-1938094026

Poems for Edna
ISBN 978-1938094033

The Burning of Bishop Nicholas Ridley
ISBN 978-1938094040

For the Love of Nine Muses
ISBN 978-1938094057

The Sonnet of Puerto: El Soneto Borincano
ISBN 978-1938094002

Too Much Wine Before Midnight Not Enough Before Noon
ISBN 978-1-938094-07-1

www.poeticon.com

www.ingramcontent.com/pod-product-compliance
Lightning Source LLC
LaVergne TN
LVHW051848080426
835512LV00018B/3133